Just Now I Feel Angry

Adrian Laurent

Copyright © 2021 by Adrian Laurent. Bradem Press, New Zealand.
ISBN 978-1-991114-00-6 (EPUB), 978-1-991114-01-3 (Paperback)

This book belongs to:

Abi loved playing with her castle and toys. Today she was excited. Abi planned a ball! People would come from across the land to celebrate Princess Lucia's birthday. There would be party games, cake, music and dancing.

The most exciting part of all was the dessert. Green Dragon would toast marshmallows for the guests. Abi was almost ready! But where was Green Dragon?

Abi looked everywhere. She found her brother Tom playing with Green Dragon outside. Tom had built a pile of dirt and leaves. Green Dragon sat on top and was filthy!

"Green Dragon is covered in dirt!" said Abi.
Abi's muscles were tight, her heart beat fast and
her fists clenched. She felt so angry.

Just now, I feel angry, thought Abi. She knew anger was a normal feeling and it was OK, but it was important to control it in a healthy way. Abi closed her eyes and counted five deep breaths. Afterward, she felt calm.

"Can I please have Green Dragon? It's special to me." said Abi.
"I'm sorry I took it without asking," said Tom.
Tom gave Green Dragon to Abi.

Abi tried to wash the dirt off. She wiped and scrubbed. She scrubbed so hard that she made a hole in Green Dragon's tummy. Abi started to feel angry again. Her face was hot and her breathing was fast. But Abi knew another way to help calm down.

Abi went to her room and sat at her desk. She loved to sit there, listen to music and draw. This was her safe space and helped her feel calm.

Abi drew pictures and tried to relax, but she kept thinking of Green Dragon and the hole. She felt so angry that she put her head in her hands and cried.

Abi's mum heard her and knelt beside her desk. Abi explained what happened.

"You should be proud for calming yourself down," said Abi's mum.
"And it's OK that it didn't quite work. It's OK to feel angry. Everyone feels angry sometimes."

"Anger is like a volcano," said Abi's mum. "Just like the smoke, fire and noise of a volcano, we feel the signs of anger. When you feel angry, your heart and breathing go faster. Your muscles are tight and your face is hot."

Sometimes anger feels small, like a volcano that rumbles but settles down. Other times the anger gets so big we can lose control, like a volcano erupting smoke and lava.

"Another great way to help calm down is to move your body. Let's both go for a walk while Tom and Dad stay home," said Abi's mum.

Abi and her mum walked in the park and Abi talked about how she felt.
"It feels better just talking about it," said Abi.

At home they found a felt heart and sewed it over the hole.
"It looks even cooler!" said Abi.
They washed Green Dragon. It was cleaner and softer than ever!

"Thanks, Mum!" Said Abi, "Now we must get ready for the ball."
The guests at the party loved having Green Dragon toast their marshmallows. Princess Lucia had the best birthday ever!

I hope you enjoyed the story.

Feedback from fantastic readers like you helps other parents find this book and give them confidence to choose it.

I would be so grateful if you could take one minute to click the link below or scan the QR code and leave your feedback:

Leave a review on Amazon.com (US)

or Amazon.co.uk (UK)

Thank you!

With Love,

Adrian Laurent

Download free activity sheets
and helpful resources.

Click Here
or scan the QR code below:

With Love,

Adrian Laurent

Collect the whole series and
learn essential social emotional life skills.

Click HERE or scan the QR code to
discover more:

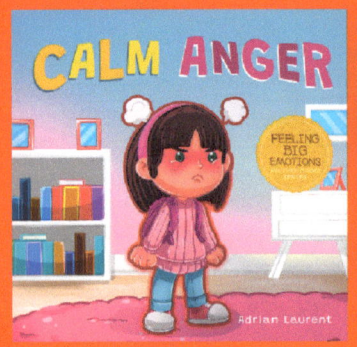
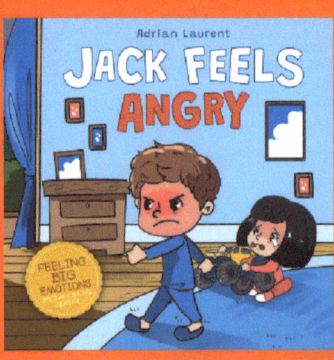
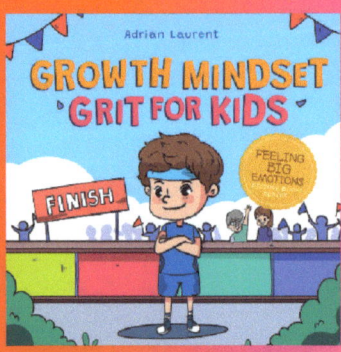
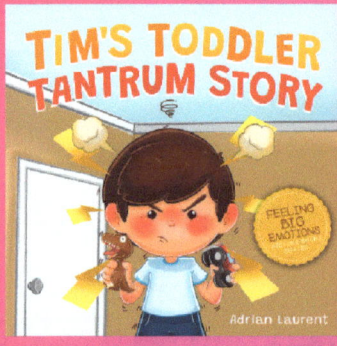

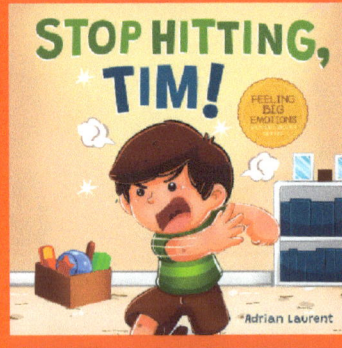
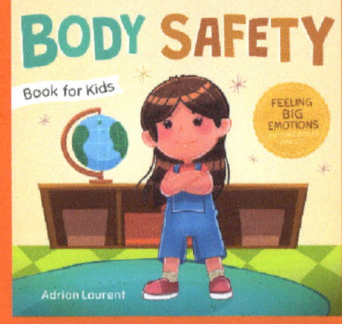
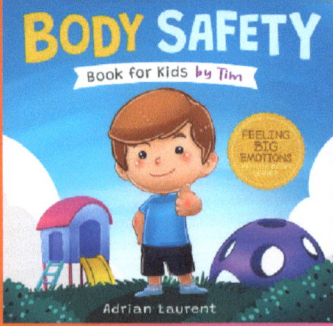
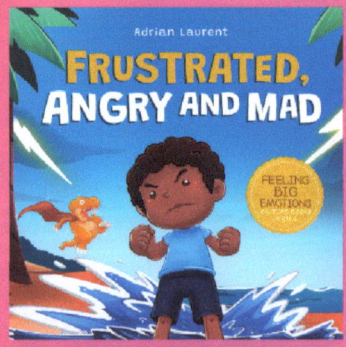

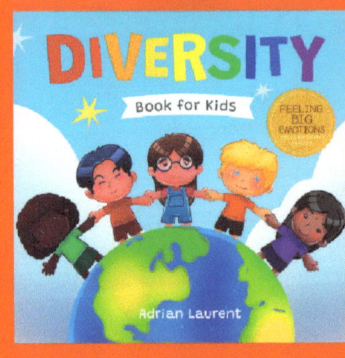
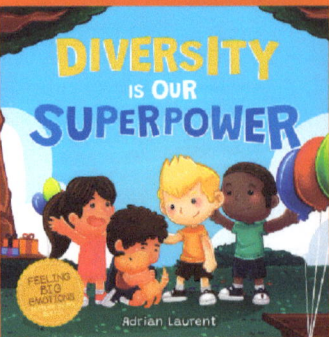
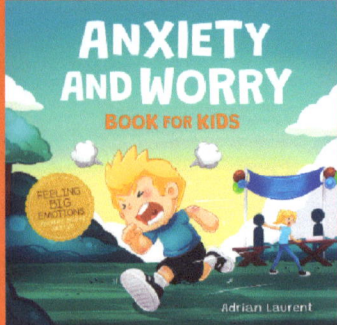

www.ingramcontent.com/pod-product-compliance
Lightning Source LLC
Chambersburg PA
CBHW041600120626
46551CB00002B/275